CADILLAC TEMPLE

HAIKU SEQUENCES BY
NORMAN SCHWENK

ALLEY PRESS

2010

Distributed by:
Parthian Books
The Old Surgery
Napier Street
Cardigan SA43 1ED
Wales, U.K.

Alley Press
2010

Published by:
Alley Press
13 Orchard Place
Cardiff CF11 9DY
Wales, U.K.

ISBN 978 1906 998 981

Book design by RX
Printed by Dalton Printers, Thesiger Street, Cardiff, U.K.

ACKNOWLEDGEMENTS

Many thanks to Richard Cox for all his work on the design of this book, and for permission to print his drawing 'Cadillac Shrine'. When I first saw this picture, at Llantarnum Grange gallery, it seemed to me that it perfectly expressed the irony of writing haiku in English.

Kikusha-ni (1753-1826) was Japanese, a Buddhist nun who became famous for her haiku and tea ceremony.

Acknowledgements are due the editors of the following publications: Poetry Wales, Presence, Roundyhouse, Scintilla and Moment of Earth: Poems and Essays in Honour of Jeremy Hooker (Celtic Publications).

Thanks to my fellow members of Edgeworks Writers' Group for their criticism and support: Jane Blank, Deborah Kay Davies, Liz Porter, Ruth Smith, Claire Syder.

And thanks to my writing buddies: Marion Glasscoe, Sue Habeshaw and Pat West.

Special thanks to my haiku mentor, Martin Lucas.

It goes without saying that none of the above bear responsibility for the final version of this book—that is mine alone.

Thanks again to Roger Ellis, especially for his riddle workshop at Ty Newydd, which showed me that the haiku is a kind of riddling poem.

Thanks to Ceri and Liz and everyone at Canton Library.

Thanks to Mike and Marie and Sarah and all at Severn Road Centre.

Finally thanks to Sarah and Gareth and Dalton Printers.

As usual my writing is full of quotes and references. Apologies first to Marion Glasscoe and Deborah Kay Davies for unconsciously nicking their phrases in my last book. And thanks to Emily Dickinson, Dizzy Gillespie, Ernest Hemingway, Randall Jarrell, D.H. Lawrence, Marcel Proust, Walt Whitman and no doubt many others.

AGAIN, FOR DEBORAH

AFTER KIKUSHA-NI (1735-1826)

is the wind Spirit?
it is like: invisible
pulling down great trees

are clouds Illusion?
they are like: hiding the road
cars appear like wraiths

is the moon Knowing?
it is like: through wind and clouds
hinting a bright face

HAIKU HELLO

nothing easier
than writing a plain haiku
and nothing harder

anything goes—that's
what I like about haiku
no subject too small

he's so observant
clever and sensitive too
so many haiku

that haiku I wrote
last night—the greatest ever
where the hell is it?

pen a prize poem
thousand quid for a haiku
reader feel the depth

AUTUMN

our gingko tree knows
the coming of autumn by
the stink of her seeds

lollipop cops bloom
bright yellow again beside
the zebra crossings

swirling whirling shapes
like schools of fish herds of sheep
starlings flock to roost

travel agent girl
puts holidays further south
up in her window

a sycamore leaf
clips the bridge of my nose on
its way to leaf-mould

BED

mysterious ship
incomprehensible home
of the prone body

worried by your wheeze
your night-breathing whistle I
realise it's mine

I move my body
against your body calming
the sad mind-rattle

dawn chorus of gulls
ak ak ak eeeee ak ak
we cuddle closer

making our bed my
hand pauses on a warm spot
beside your pillow

BIRDS

at the cathedral
inside a bronze crown of thorns
five swallows nesting

seagulls dance on grass
mimic the beat of raindrops
and up pops breakfast

a black kite swings high
some invisible trapeze
people oooh and ahhh

walking the canal
a heron stands and peers round
keeping just ahead

that magpie again
he's selling The Big Issue
at your kitchen door

BODY

body-embossing
in pink faux-Celtic patterns
when she turns in bed

bang! she drops the soap
through the shower curtain slips
a dimply bottom

the way she hunches
her back to reach the mirror
doing her makeup

she studies her face
in a brass doorplate across
the quiet arcade

snap of snooker balls
she leans over the table
her breasts in the way

BOOKS

read to me daddy
she's perched on granny's afghan
putting off bedtime

spiderman listens
draped across his mother's lap
he's in the story

books breed like bunnies
hop on top of each other
take over your home

she crosses on the
red light laughing lost in a
Garrison Keillor

I talk to a box
it tells me I owe sixty
pence library fines

BUGS

first lunch alfresco
first wasp homes in on thermals
of white burgundy

those coffee-ground mounds
of waste dirt the ants tip round
are growing again

butterflies of night
why do we dislike them so?
flippity brown flaps

buzz buzz buzz buzz buzz
month of the mad dying fly
Emily swat it!

backstage spider—she
keeps her big web working right
up to the panto

CAFÉ

nemesis enters
looking like a complete dweeb
so gratifying

at the next table
a small boy bops in his chair
rolling arms and eyes

clatter and chatter
that's what makes a good café
a peaceable buzz

young Asian women
making sounds in their language
signing in silence

drinks in the garden
smiling friends perfect weather
enter nemesis

CALENDAR

Jaffa oranges
in January—seasons
have been deleted

O now it's April
when tax forms flap on the mat
who'd be in England?

cardie off showing
her bare bump—what she was up
to in October

you know it's autumn
when the bloom is on the sloe
and someone's picked them

she loves November
sheltering from the weather
the warmth of his back

DEAD

after the mugging
she asks have I got her purse?
again and again

I can see him sweat
he thinks if I lie for him
he'll escape the war

stove-in car steaming
ambulance man on his mike
someone still inside

clearing the office
haunted by your messages
voices on standby

shredding documents
white feathers in the hen house
where a skunk has browsed

DINNER

sparkling rosé
like jumping in a puddle
when you're about three

such good companions
fresh tomato and basil
cool beside the pool

an honest claret
warm breeze from the Sahara
without that red dust

a much-loved grandma
telling your favourite stories
rosemary roast lamb

chocolate possesses
a spiritual dimension
we thank God for life

DISGUSTING

it falls in the loo
will you reach in to fetch it
or stand there gawping?

watching her eat chips
politically incorrect
feelings take over

changing their nappies
why is it less repellent
when they're your own kids?

the President on
TV calmly hunting a
bogey with his thumb

they fart in bed now
is it the end of romance
or the beginning?

DRIVING

driving 70
cruising along beside us
a flock of nine swans

gold morning sun lights
the face of the driver in
my rear-view mirror

Just AAsk tow truck guy
struggles to start a Robin
not-so Reliant

stress-free travel bus
converts front of silver merc
into used tinfoil

stop smell the roses
if poets can't be bothered
then whoever will?

EAST

the serious men
at Bilal Mosque visibly
cheer up when it rains

the Buddhist in me
challenged by a small squirmy
white worm in the tub

Eurasian waitress
stops to light a cigarette
Hopper should paint her

Sumo wrestler knows
how to display dignity
naked on his butt

the better you are
I'm talking about Tai Chi
the slower you are

FAN

watching Wimbledon
my neighbour screams just like that
an orgastic cat

the retired boxer
looks like a dentist but I
still hear the gloves whop

stay in the moment
says top golfer Justin Rose
could he mean haiku?

big match abandoned
but does the double rainbow
promise new cricket?

watching the footie
they never score until you
go to the toilet

FENNEL

a sniff of fennel
and he's a small boy munching
liquorice cigars

and then a big boy
chewing on plug tobacco
laced with aniseed

and so a young man
watching ouzo go cloudy
everything gets blurred

then in middle age
strung out—hitting the absinthe
hallucinogen

now in sage old age
a flavour in his garden
the scent of fennel

FLAT

discouraging smells
emanate from God knows where
musty yet dusty

our landlord is in
denial about those dark
frisbee-size damp spots

wood laminate floors
that curdle up and crackle
new they looked so fine

cold tap that slams shut
never mind—the hot tap will
run lashings of cold

and when the household
slurry bubbles the wrong way
poopy patio

FRIEND

cheers you say and go
ahead of us the way you
did on weekend walks

we meet at the church
dedicated not to God
but to a writer

forget little urns
your ash comes in a big box
slippery gritty

boosting our bluebells
in the Wood of the Gentry
but I miss your laugh

we read your poems
in a clean well-lighted place
your book sells like beer

GARDEN

it starts early March
this battle for the hostas
slugs and snails and us

our luscious herb bed
rooting out the wild nettles
my gloved hands tingle

wiping spit balls off
bronze fennel—a lady bug
were they her dinner?

valerian and
foxglove spring out of stone walls
triumphs of neglect

dilapidated
we try to imagine how
it will grow again

HAPPY

your voice trumpeting
you've won the premium bonds
joyful trivia

a Muslim woman
discreetly lifts her veil to
eat a banana

a little girl's face
above her father's shoulder
never been so high

this darkened wine bar
lit candles on the tables
packed with customers

texting each other
like passing secret notes in
the back row at school

HOUSEHUSBAND

riverside market
shoppers in search of flavour
ignore spring drizzle

the mould retreating
the dust bunnies attacking
swings and roundabouts

jangle of hangers
tells him what the next job is
video ironing

butterflies of night
the iron entered his soul when
they chumbled his tweed

stepping on the scales
the surest sign of winter
half a stone of fat

INFURIATING

he says he's sorry
she says he says sorry too
much—he says sorry

excluded from some
club you never wanted to
be a member of

the pop tune you heard
in a shop somewhere that stays
in your head all day

people who say men
are made better than women
and blame it on God

the dead sincere look
in a politician's eye
when he starts to lie

KIDS

in spite of the bad
smells made by the media
he still smiles at kids

with their granddad at
the playground confronted by
Telegraphreaders

two little mixed-race
kids are made to testify
for this old white guy

our fruit and veg shop
is chock-a-block with pushchairs
so you can't get in

everyone frightened
where's the space to bang around ?
who'd be a kid now?

LISTEN

I listen to my
white scream at 4 thousand hertz
then I don't listen

easy so easy
sighs the bendy bus easing
its ramp to the kerb

great clumps of blue grass
in the herbaceous border
whispering music

moment of silence
the conductor cups her hand
the choir holds its breath

2 a.m. shouting
but we can't call the police
it is the police

LOOK

the back of her neck
makes him want to cry now she's
cut her hair shorter

her old friend seems strange
gold earring and clean-shaven
marriage makeover

blonde librarian
tattoo inside her cleavage
he tries not to stare

off to college soon
he adjusts the wing mirror
gives his hair a flick

he blouses his shirt
vainly hoping she won't clock
the old food locker

MONEY

I miss the sixpence
it isn't just nostalgia
yes it is—why not?

tills rang little bells
today computers snarl up
our queues grow longer

who invented cash?
and who invented credit?
cash that isn't there?

it doesn't feel real
until you run out of it
then the tone changes

big bill for water
almost every day it rains
pennies from heaven

MOVIE

why have I spent so
much of my time witnessing
actors pretend things?

we are not actors
don't want to go down in flames
with people watching

the twin towers shown
as an establishing shot
saddens many films

the Empire State used
as an action location
gladdens many too

so why do I cry
when Kong turns to the sunrise
softly thumps his chest?

NIPPLE

'clitoris is the
only human organ made
solely for pleasure'

says The Vagina
Monologues—so what about
his pointless nipples?

'useless as tits on
a boar' declares the farmer
but sows caress them

with their bristly backs
waking the spiral penis
to full arousal

in the shower his
nipples are erect and still
tender from last night

NORTH/SOUTH

beer and greasy chips
that's what we like in the North
and pass the cream buns

dressing our best we
go out in the wind and rain
fashion blows away

they lounge on corners
wearing the latest clobber
and effortless tans

cook with virgin oil
(but what is extra virgin—
are you one or not?)

stuff that's good for you
that's what they like in the South
so pass the vino

QUINTET

Quintet by Brahms who
played in brothels whose beard smelled
of smoking stogies

we remark how much
the pianist resembles
a bank manager

the violins wear
shiny suits like footballers
huge collars and ties

the viola has
pitted skin the cello long
bare sinewy arms

these be our gods who
make the music of Heaven
we patter our palms

RAIN

rain on the lean-to
roof makes light skittering sounds
tip-toeing rats' feet

lost in thought he stands
under the bus shelter just
where rain is leaking

a little afraid
waterfall roar on skylights
everyone looks up

silent rivulets
on the glass—we play a game
of raindrop races

after the dry spell
rain silvering our roof slates
reflects a full moon

REPETITIONS

if you love someone
you love their repetitions
who said that? Twain? Proust?

mornings when she says
there's something wrong with me I
can't seem to wake up

and when she's making
herself more lovely—what's more
important than that?

now I watch her brain
tick-ticking trying to keep
everyone happy

and when she says I
can't seem to get to sleep just
before zuzzing off

RIDDLES

nose with giant horn
any moment apt to charge
yes—an SUV

thick shell front and back
suddenly its head is gone
—a politician

loves shiny prizes
voice like a football rattle
magpie?—game show host

forked fluttering tongue
skin-sloughing coiling body
—a philanderer

it's better than you
way higher up the food chain
you can't guess—a worm

RINGS

grandfather's gold ring
two naked ladies embrace
the family jewels

inscribed Kate to Pete
she also gave him a lead
bullet in the heart

toxic wedding ring
how do you get rid of it?
flog it? Oxfam it?

shopping for a ring
heads bowed—the tiny circle
maybe they're lucky

a sandalwood box
and inside a sapphire blue
as the evening star

SAD

your voice sounds husky
you've lost your keys pranged the car
tragic trivia

his therapist looks
as if she needs therapy
this sunny morning

badminton shuttle
made for flight and excitement
rolls in the gutter

a darkened wine bar
lit candles on the tables
waiters fold napkins

I think our signal
is breaking up but now it
sounds like you sobbing

SCARY

he forgets his hat
fine soft rain feathers his pate
the Chernobyl cloud

you blanch at the news
sorry I bought a paper
I turn to the jobs

that dream where you dump
hugely in somebody's loo
then can't flush it down

dog-pecker gnats drift
in the bright middle distance
behind my eyelids

yesterday feeling
ready to die—today this
grovelling terror

SEE

this is your blind spot
says the optician pointing
to a big black hole

seeing upside down
your brain turns it right side up
how clever is that?

draw it upside down
says the art teacher laughing
use your right-side brain

my view out Van Gogh's
window is flat and banal
compared with his view

were we about six?
the girl I played doctor with
is going blind now

SHOPS

PDSA shop
sign in blue on the front door
we're sorry no dogs

nearly comes off his
bike avoiding a heron
in front of ASDA

it's Wally's deli
floor to ceiling every wall
cave of no-no food

an old romantic
he still takes the price tag off
her Tesco lilies

Christian bookshop now
Mrs Foster's house the last
brothel in our town

SMELL

coffee aroma
hangs over the walk floating
you into the shop

real summer's arrived
lots of scented female flesh
B.O. on the bus

filthy street fragrant
with linden seed and privet
after evening rain

in the cinema
we watch Perfume but nearby
some ass is farting

new moon and low cloud
hovering black trees and sharp
smell of fresh-cut grass

SOUL

smears spitballs splodges
it's only paint on paper
yet we stand in awe

roomful of poets
one of those rare evenings you
feel chuffed to be one

empty theatre
shrivelled souls with tickets show
we're sat in their seats

you sing beside me
I echo and resound like
a proud organ pipe

big yawns and little
swallowing noises when we
drink tea in the dark

SPRING

he hears her key turn
in the lock while it's still light
after months of dark

the first weeds of spring
non-smokers join smokers out
in front of the pub

a shadow of His
hand cast by hard April light
palm open thumb up

this tiny rain there's
no name for that only falls
at cricket matches

so bright you need shades
these banks of sun-care products
in the big drug store

SUMMER

brushing last summer's
sandals with a J-cloth—puffs
of winter mildew

my Panama hat
waits in the airing cupboard
for his day to dawn

blinding heat—Celts then
Romans worshipped water here
made the place holy

after Evensong
we chat in the beer garden
over G and Ts

we lie on the grass
watching out for shooting stars
why do we do that?

SURPRISING

vanilla extract
sweet come-on aroma then
a slap in the face

beneath the blackthorn's
frozen dead-white explosion
our mouths fall open

dual carriageway
Lytton-Strachey-look-alike
unicycling

that brunette on the
bar stool has no panties on
her tan goes right up

vomit smell followed
by fully blessed-out taste buds
viva parmesan

TASTE

sinus infection
all night a sweaty army
marches through your mouth

but a good taste is
water when you are thirsty
and there is no taste

steak is like sex—when
it's good it's great—when it's not
so good it's still good

I celebrate cheese
crumbly chalky Caerphilly
earthy creamy goat's

tang of peaty smoke
Glen-something-or-other malt
but wasted on me

TOUCH

numb feet—rare syndrome
afflicting fitness freaks not
lazy folk like me

stroking Harriet
her ginger coat still thick soft
knobbly backbone though

you give me a hug
sadness falls away like a
boa constrictor

a needle of glass
skewers wadded newspaper
OK here's the blood

tip-toeing on cold
bathroom tiles in the blank dark
wait—is that a slug?

UNIFORM

going off to work
her puritan uniform
defeats its object

breasts straining in blue
gabardine—sensational
legs in sheer black tights

black leather court shoes
pushing up calves and buttocks
while slimming the foot

the total effect
is smart severe and trashy
discipline mistress

you said it Randy
we can't conceal the leopard
in dull null navy

WAITING

waiting is like jail
somebody keeps you locked up
you squirm in your shell

he waits in the bar
she waits in the restaurant
they miss each other

fabulous stone egg
laid by a real Welsh dragon
you've had a long wait

M & S queueing
she waits and pays attention
to being alive

waiting is useful
and loafing too—the best things
hatch from sitting still

WALK

haiku hike with friends
is the chat more interesting
than the poetry?

if you didn't know
would you believe the moon makes
the tidal creek high?

is she diminished
or enhanced by my haiku ?
dot in the distance?

is the ninth wave big?
I watch and count all morning
till my shoes get wet

a walk to the beach
and back with a lovely shell
rubbish poem though

WEST

walking to prayers he
glares at her decolletage
stones her with his eyes

his Cadillac wants
to look as if it's flying
even when it's parked

she makes her X and
slots it in the tin hoping
it's not a waste bin

new porcelain room
bathtub toilet sink bidet
envy of the street

coughing till your ribs
hurt to breathe—a flu bug that
wasn't in the jab

WINDOW

a three-legged cat
galloping past our window
at least I think so

yellow street lighting
makes their faces hideous
just for a moment

woman with MS
unsteady but she's going
shopping looking chic

window box meadow
long blond grasses toss their hair
behind wooden blinds

the radio sings
through the air a lone snowflake
silently descends

WINTER

our West Indian
band warms up winter mornings
boiler pipes and rads

some Xmas decs flash
and glitter making sadder
the sad waiting room

I kick the giraffe's
neck back against the bottom
of the draughty door

a little boy leaps
lopes to stay in his father's
footprints through the snow

their football hero
wears an extra pair of socks
and his wife's old tights

HAIKU FAREWELL

reflexive haiku
see the poem disappear
straight up its own ass

sipping the Shiraz
together waiting for lunch
writing a haiku

one-coffee haiku
not the grinding ordeal of
two or even three

like a vol-au-vent
anything goes in haiku
why always chicken?

think I'll go downtown
have a walk do some shopping
fed up with haiku